A
Christian Delight
Directed
Curriculum
K-2

90 Guided Lessons

By Laura Warden

Instructions

In this book your student will learn all the basics such as, reading, writing and spelling. Your student will be introduced to 90 of Frys sight words.

Along with your own math curriculum and phonics program you will have a complete 90 day curriculum.

It is a delight directed book which allows the student to choose topics and books they love and use those to learn with. Every person is unique and different and we should as teachers embrace every learning style because God has created everyone to be unique in his or her own way.

Parent Tip: If your student has a hard time writing for the story pages then have your student tell you the story while you write it down for them.

I praise you, for I am fearfully and wonderfully made. Wonderful are your works; my soul knows it very well. Psalm 139:14

This Book Belongs To:

Name:_____

Grade:_____

Date:_____

Choose Your Books

Books about animals

_____

_____

_____

_____

_____

Books about bugs

_____

_____

_____

_____

_____

Books about Letters and Words

_____

_____

_____

_____

_____

Story Books/History/Science

_____

_____

_____

Choose your own math curriculum, phonics program
and story book bible.
When you finish these books just choose some more!

Day 1   Name:_____

Bible

Have an adult read you a bible story from your
bible draw a picture of what you learned.

Math

Practice counting to 100 color each square as you count.

Hundreds Chart

1	2	3	4	5	6	7	8	9	10
11	12	13	14	15	16	17	18	19	20
21	22	23	24	25	26	27	28	29	30
31	32	33	34	35	36	37	38	39	40
41	42	43	44	45	46	47	48	49	50
51	52	53	54	55	56	57	58	59	60
61	62	63	64	65	66	67	68	69	70
71	72	73	74	75	76	77	78	79	80
81	82	83	84	85	86	87	88	89	90
91	92	93	94	95	96	97	98	99	100

Reading
Choose a book and have an adult read for 10 min. to you
or you can read for 10 min. to an adult

What did you read about today?
Draw a picture of what you read.

Writing and Spelling
Sight Words

Read	Trace	Write
the	the	
of	of	
and	and	
a	a	
to	you	

Copy Work
copy the sentence and draw a picture

The rat sat.

Color the picture

Wooly Mammoth

Day 2   **Name:**_____

Bible
Have an adult read you a bible story from your bible draw a picture of what you learned.

Math

Practice counting to 100 color each square as you count.

Hundreds Chart

1	2	3	4	5	6	7	8	9	10
11	12	13	14	15	16	17	18	19	20
21	22	23	24	25	26	27	28	29	30
31	32	33	34	35	36	37	38	39	40
41	42	43	44	45	46	47	48	49	50
51	52	53	54	55	56	57	58	59	60
61	62	63	64	65	66	67	68	69	70
71	72	73	74	75	76	77	78	79	80
81	82	83	84	85	86	87	88	89	90
91	92	93	94	95	96	97	98	99	100

Reading
Choose a book and have an adult read for 10 min. to you
or you can read for 10 min. to an adult

What did you read about today?
Draw a picture of what you read.

Writing and Spelling
Sight Words

Read	Trace	Write
in	in	
is	is	
you	you	
that	that	
it	it	

Copy Work
copy the sentence and draw a picture

That cat is fat.

Color the picture
Cat

Day 3   Name _____

<u>Bible</u>
Have an adult read you a bible story from your
bible draw a picture of what you learned.

Math

Practice counting to 100 color each square as you count.

Hundreds Chart

1	2	3	4	5	6	7	8	9	10
11	12	13	14	15	16	17	18	19	20
21	22	23	24	25	26	27	28	29	30
31	32	33	34	35	36	37	38	39	40
41	42	43	44	45	46	47	48	49	50
51	52	53	54	55	56	57	58	59	60
61	62	63	64	65	66	67	68	69	70
71	72	73	74	75	76	77	78	79	80
81	82	83	84	85	86	87	88	89	90
91	92	93	94	95	96	97	98	99	100

Reading
Choose a book and have an adult read for 10 min. to you
or you can read for 10 min. to an adult

What did you read about today?
Draw a picture of what you read.

Writing and Spelling
Sight Words

Read	Trace	Write
he	he	
was	was	
for	for	
on	on	
are	are	

Copy Work
copy the sentence and draw a picture

He was a tall man.

Color the picture
Eagle

Day 4   Name:_____

Bible

Have an adult read you a bible story from your
bible draw a picture of what you learned.

Math
Practice counting to 100 color each square as you count.

Hundreds Chart

1	2	3	4	5	6	7	8	9	10
11	12	13	14	15	16	17	18	19	20
21	22	23	24	25	26	27	28	29	30
31	32	33	34	35	36	37	38	39	40
41	42	43	44	45	46	47	48	49	50
51	52	53	54	55	56	57	58	59	60
61	62	63	64	65	66	67	68	69	70
71	72	73	74	75	76	77	78	79	80
81	82	83	84	85	86	87	88	89	90
91	92	93	94	95	96	97	98	99	100

Reading
Choose a book and have an adult read for 10 min. to you
or you can read for 10 min. to an adult

What did you read about today?
Draw a picture of what you read.

Writing and Spelling
Sight Words

Read	Trace	Write
as	as	
with	with	
his	his	
they	they	
I	I	

Copy Work
copy the sentence and draw a picture

I like his dog.

Color the picture
Canadian Goose

Day 5   Name:_____

Bible
Have an adult read you a bible story from your bible draw a picture of what you learned.

Math

Practice counting to 100 color each square as you count.

Hundreds Chart

1	2	3	4	5	6	7	8	9	10
11	12	13	14	15	16	17	18	19	20
21	22	23	24	25	26	27	28	29	30
31	32	33	34	35	36	37	38	39	40
41	42	43	44	45	46	47	48	49	50
51	52	53	54	55	56	57	58	59	60
61	62	63	64	65	66	67	68	69	70
71	72	73	74	75	76	77	78	79	80
81	82	83	84	85	86	87	88	89	90
91	92	93	94	95	96	97	98	99	100

Reading
Choose a book and have an adult read for 10 min. to you
or you can read for 10 min. to an adult

What did you read about today?
Draw a picture of what you read.

Writing and Spelling
Sight Words

Read	Trace	Write
at	at	
be	be	
this	this	
have	have	
from	from	

Copy Work
copy the sentence and draw a picture

The rat is from the barn.

Color the picture
Elephant

Day 6   Name:_____

Bible

Have an adult read you a bible story from your
bible draw a picture of what you learned.

Math

Practice skip counting by 2's

Color the squares as you count have an adult help you.

Hundreds Chart

1	2	3	4	5	6	7	8	9	10
11	12	13	14	15	16	17	18	19	20
21	22	23	24	25	26	27	28	29	30
31	32	33	34	35	36	37	38	39	40
41	42	43	44	45	46	47	48	49	50
51	52	53	54	55	56	57	58	59	60
61	62	63	64	65	66	67	68	69	70
71	72	73	74	75	76	77	78	79	80
81	82	83	84	85	86	87	88	89	90
91	92	93	94	95	96	97	98	99	100

Reading
Choose a book and have an adult read for 10 min. to you
or you can read for 10 min. to an adult

What did you read about today?
Draw a picture of what you read.

Writing and Spelling
Sight Words

Read	Trace	Write
or	or	
one	one	
had	had	
by	by	
words	words	

Copy Work
copy the sentence and draw a picture

One cat had fleas.

Color the picture
Lion

Day 7   **Name:**_____

Bible
Have an adult read you a bible story from your
bible draw a picture of what you learned.

Math
Practice skip counting by 2's
Color the squares as you count have an adult help you.

Hundreds Chart

1	2	3	4	5	6	7	8	9	10
11	12	13	14	15	16	17	18	19	20
21	22	23	24	25	26	27	28	29	30
31	32	33	34	35	36	37	38	39	40
41	42	43	44	45	46	47	48	49	50
51	52	53	54	55	56	57	58	59	60
61	62	63	64	65	66	67	68	69	70
71	72	73	74	75	76	77	78	79	80
81	82	83	84	85	86	87	88	89	90
91	92	93	94	95	96	97	98	99	100

Reading
Choose a book and have an adult read for 10 min. to you
or you can read for 10 min. to an adult

What did you read about today?
Draw a picture of what you read.

Writing and Spelling
Sight Words

Read	Trace	Write
but	but	
not	not	
what	what	
all	all	
were	were	

Copy Work
copy the sentence and draw a picture

All the dogs were happy.

Color the picture

Tiger

Day 8   **Name:**_____

Bible
Have an adult read you a bible story from your bible draw a picture of what you learned.

Math
Practice skip counting by 2's
Color the squares as you count have an adult help you.

Hundreds Chart

1	2	3	4	5	6	7	8	9	10
11	12	13	14	15	16	17	18	19	20
21	22	23	24	25	26	27	28	29	30
31	32	33	34	35	36	37	38	39	40
41	42	43	44	45	46	47	48	49	50
51	52	53	54	55	56	57	58	59	60
61	62	63	64	65	66	67	68	69	70
71	72	73	74	75	76	77	78	79	80
81	82	83	84	85	86	87	88	89	90
91	92	93	94	95	96	97	98	99	100

Reading
Choose a book and have an adult read for 10 min. to you
or you can read for 10 min. to an adult

What did you read about today?
Draw a picture of what you read.

Writing and Spelling
Sight Words

Read	Trace	Write
we	we	
when	when	
your	your	
can	can	
said	said	

Copy Work
copy the sentence and draw a picture

Your dog can run fast.

Color the picture
Sea turtle

Day 9   Name:_____

Bible

Have an adult read you a bible story from your bible draw a picture of what you learned.

Math

Practice skip counting by 2's
Color the squares as you count have an adult help you.

Hundreds Chart

1	2	3	4	5	6	7	8	9	10
11	12	13	14	15	16	17	18	19	20
21	22	23	24	25	26	27	28	29	30
31	32	33	34	35	36	37	38	39	40
41	42	43	44	45	46	47	48	49	50
51	52	53	54	55	56	57	58	59	60
61	62	63	64	65	66	67	68	69	70
71	72	73	74	75	76	77	78	79	80
81	82	83	84	85	86	87	88	89	90
91	92	93	94	95	96	97	98	99	100

Reading

Choose a book and have an adult read for 10 min. to you
or you can read for 10 min. to an adult

What did you read about today?
Draw a picture of what you read.

Writing and Spelling
Sight Words

Read	Trace	Write
there	there	
use	use	
an	an	
each	each	
which	which	

Copy Work
copy the sentence and draw a picture

Each rat is fat.

Color the picture
Pig

Day 10   Name:_____

Bible
Have an adult read you a bible story from your
bible draw a picture of what you learned.

Math

Practice skip counting by 2's
Color the squares as you count have an adult help you.

Hundreds Chart

1	2	3	4	5	6	7	8	9	10
11	12	13	14	15	16	17	18	19	20
21	22	23	24	25	26	27	28	29	30
31	32	33	34	35	36	37	38	39	40
41	42	43	44	45	46	47	48	49	50
51	52	53	54	55	56	57	58	59	60
61	62	63	64	65	66	67	68	69	70
71	72	73	74	75	76	77	78	79	80
81	82	83	84	85	86	87	88	89	90
91	92	93	94	95	96	97	98	99	100

<u>Reading</u>
Choose a book and have an adult read for 10 min. to you or you can read for 10 min. to an adult

What did you read about today?
Draw a picture of what you read.

Writing and Spelling
Sight Words

Read	Trace	Write
she	she	
do	do	
how	how	
their	their	
if	if	

Copy Work
copy the sentence and draw a picture

She had a red hat.

Color the picture
Zebra

Day 11   Name:_____

Bible

Have an adult read you a bible story from your bible draw a picture of what you learned.

Math
Practice skip counting by 5's
Color the squares as you count have an adult help you.

Hundreds Chart

1	2	3	4	5	6	7	8	9	10
11	12	13	14	15	16	17	18	19	20
21	22	23	24	25	26	27	28	29	30
31	32	33	34	35	36	37	38	39	40
41	42	43	44	45	46	47	48	49	50
51	52	53	54	55	56	57	58	59	60
61	62	63	64	65	66	67	68	69	70
71	72	73	74	75	76	77	78	79	80
81	82	83	84	85	86	87	88	89	90
91	92	93	94	95	96	97	98	99	100

Reading
Choose a book and have an adult read for 10 min. to you
or you can read for 10 min. to an adult

What did you read about today?
Draw a picture of what you read.

Writing and Spelling
Sight Words

Read	Trace	Write
will	will	
up	up	
other	other	
about	about	
out	out	

Copy Work
copy the sentence and draw a picture

I will clean up.

Color the picture
Dolphin

Day 12   Name_____

Bible
Have an adult read you a bible story from your
bible draw a picture of what you learned.

Math
Practice skip counting by 5's
Color the squares as you count have an adult help you.

Hundreds Chart

1	2	3	4	5	6	7	8	9	10
11	12	13	14	15	16	17	18	19	20
21	22	23	24	25	26	27	28	29	30
31	32	33	34	35	36	37	38	39	40
41	42	43	44	45	46	47	48	49	50
51	52	53	54	55	56	57	58	59	60
61	62	63	64	65	66	67	68	69	70
71	72	73	74	75	76	77	78	79	80
81	82	83	84	85	86	87	88	89	90
91	92	93	94	95	96	97	98	99	100

Reading
Choose a book and have an adult read for 10 min. to you
or you can read for 10 min. to an adult

What did you read about today?
Draw a picture of what you read.

Writing and Spelling
Sight Words

Read	Trace	Write
many	many	
then	then	
them	them	
these	these	
so	so	

Copy Work
copy the sentence and draw a picture

These apples are red.

Color the picture
Ox

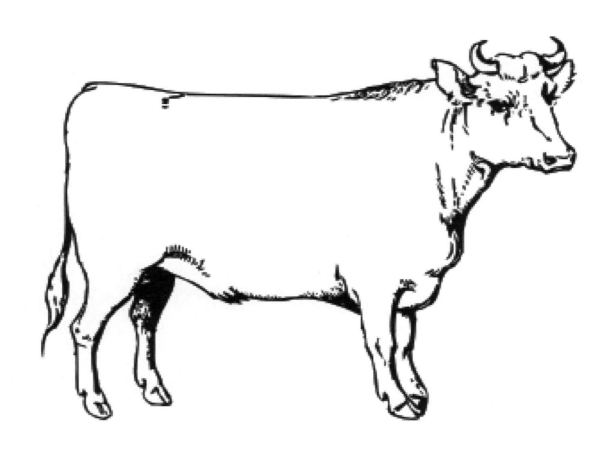

Day 13   Name_____

Bible
Have an adult read you a bible story from your
bible draw a picture of what you learned.

Math
Practice skip counting by 5's
Color the squares as you count have an adult help you.

Hundreds Chart

1	2	3	4	5	6	7	8	9	10
11	12	13	14	15	16	17	18	19	20
21	22	23	24	25	26	27	28	29	30
31	32	33	34	35	36	37	38	39	40
41	42	43	44	45	46	47	48	49	50
51	52	53	54	55	56	57	58	59	60
61	62	63	64	65	66	67	68	69	70
71	72	73	74	75	76	77	78	79	80
81	82	83	84	85	86	87	88	89	90
91	92	93	94	95	96	97	98	99	100

Reading
Choose a book and have an adult read for 10 min. to you
or you can read for 10 min. to an adult

What did you read about today?
Draw a picture of what you read.

Writing and Spelling
Sight Words

Read	Trace	Write
some	some	
her	her	
would	would	
make	make	
like	like	

Copy Work
copy the sentence and draw a picture

I like to bake.

Color the picture
Hen

Day 14   Name_____

Bible

Have an adult read you a bible story from your
bible draw a picture of what you learned.

Math
Practice skip counting by 5's
Color the squares as you count have an adult help you.

Hundreds Chart

1	2	3	4	5	6	7	8	9	10
11	12	13	14	15	16	17	18	19	20
21	22	23	24	25	26	27	28	29	30
31	32	33	34	35	36	37	38	39	40
41	42	43	44	45	46	47	48	49	50
51	52	53	54	55	56	57	58	59	60
61	62	63	64	65	66	67	68	69	70
71	72	73	74	75	76	77	78	79	80
81	82	83	84	85	86	87	88	89	90
91	92	93	94	95	96	97	98	99	100

Reading
Choose a book and have an adult read for 10 min. to you or you can read for 10 min. to an adult

What did you read about today?
Draw a picture of what you read.

Writing and Spelling
Sight Words

Read	Trace	Write
him	him	
into	into	
time	time	
has	has	
look	look	

Copy Work
copy the sentence and draw a picture

Look at the time.

Color the picture
Butterfly

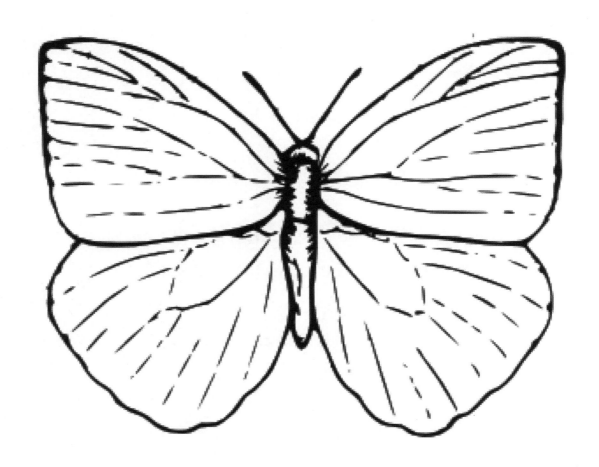

Day 15   Name_____

Bible

Have an adult read you a bible story from your
bible draw a picture of what you learned.

Math

Practice skip counting by 5's
Color the squares as you count have an adult help you.

Hundreds Chart

1	2	3	4	5	6	7	8	9	10
11	12	13	14	15	16	17	18	19	20
21	22	23	24	25	26	27	28	29	30
31	32	33	34	35	36	37	38	39	40
41	42	43	44	45	46	47	48	49	50
51	52	53	54	55	56	57	58	59	60
61	62	63	64	65	66	67	68	69	70
71	72	73	74	75	76	77	78	79	80
81	82	83	84	85	86	87	88	89	90
91	92	93	94	95	96	97	98	99	100

Reading
Choose a book and have an adult read for 10 min. to you
or you can read for 10 min. to an adult

What did you read about today?
Draw a picture of what you read.

Writing and Spelling
Sight Words

Read	Trace	Write
two	two	
more	more	
write	write	
go	go	
see	see	

Copy Work
copy the sentence and draw a picture

I see two hats.

Color the picture
Dog

Day 16　　　　**Name**_____

Bible
Have an adult read you a bible story from your
bible draw a picture of what you learned.

Math
Practice skip counting by 10's
Color the squares as you count have an adult help you.

Hundreds Chart

1	2	3	4	5	6	7	8	9	10
11	12	13	14	15	16	17	18	19	20
21	22	23	24	25	26	27	28	29	30
31	32	33	34	35	36	37	38	39	40
41	42	43	44	45	46	47	48	49	50
51	52	53	54	55	56	57	58	59	60
61	62	63	64	65	66	67	68	69	70
71	72	73	74	75	76	77	78	79	80
81	82	83	84	85	86	87	88	89	90
91	92	93	94	95	96	97	98	99	100

Reading
Choose a book and have an adult read for 10 min. to you
or you can read for 10 min. to an adult

What did you read about today?
Draw a picture of what you read.

Writing and Spelling
Sight Words

Read	Trace	Write
number	number	
no	no	
way	way	
could	could	
people	people	

Copy Work
copy the sentence and draw a picture

I like the number two.

Color the picture
Bull Frog

Day 17   Name_____

Bible

Have an adult read you a bible story from your
bible draw a picture of what you learned.

Math
Practice skip counting by 10's
Color the squares as you count have an adult help you.

Hundreds Chart

1	2	3	4	5	6	7	8	9	10
11	12	13	14	15	16	17	18	19	20
21	22	23	24	25	26	27	28	29	30
31	32	33	34	35	36	37	38	39	40
41	42	43	44	45	46	47	48	49	50
51	52	53	54	55	56	57	58	59	60
61	62	63	64	65	66	67	68	69	70
71	72	73	74	75	76	77	78	79	80
81	82	83	84	85	86	87	88	89	90
91	92	93	94	95	96	97	98	99	100

Reading
Choose a book and have an adult read for 10 min. to you
or you can read for 10 min. to an adult

What did you read about today?
Draw a picture of what you read.

Writing and Spelling
Sight Words

Read	Trace	Write
my	my	
than	than	
first	first	
water	water	
been	been	

Copy Work
copy the sentence and draw a picture

My cat needs water.

Color the picture
Horse

Day 18   Name_____

Bible
Have an adult read you a bible story from your bible draw a picture of what you learned.

Math
Practice skip counting by 10's
Color the squares as you count have an adult help you.

Hundreds Chart

1	2	3	4	5	6	7	8	9	10
11	12	13	14	15	16	17	18	19	20
21	22	23	24	25	26	27	28	29	30
31	32	33	34	35	36	37	38	39	40
41	42	43	44	45	46	47	48	49	50
51	52	53	54	55	56	57	58	59	60
61	62	63	64	65	66	67	68	69	70
71	72	73	74	75	76	77	78	79	80
81	82	83	84	85	86	87	88	89	90
91	92	93	94	95	96	97	98	99	100

<u>Reading</u>
Choose a book and have an adult read for 10 min. to you
or you can read for 10 min. to an adult

What did you read about today?
Draw a picture of what you read.

Writing and Spelling
Sight Words

Read	Trace	Write
called	called	
who	who	
am	am	
its	its	
now	now	

Copy Work
copy the sentence and draw a picture

I am happy.

Color the picture
Sea Horse

Day 19   Name_____

<u>Bible</u>
Have an adult read you a bible story from your
bible draw a picture of what you learned.

Math
Practice skip counting by 10's
Color the squares as you count have an adult help you.

Hundreds Chart

1	2	3	4	5	6	7	8	9	10
11	12	13	14	15	16	17	18	19	20
21	22	23	24	25	26	27	28	29	30
31	32	33	34	35	36	37	38	39	40
41	42	43	44	45	46	47	48	49	50
51	52	53	54	55	56	57	58	59	60
61	62	63	64	65	66	67	68	69	70
71	72	73	74	75	76	77	78	79	80
81	82	83	84	85	86	87	88	89	90
91	92	93	94	95	96	97	98	99	100

Reading

Choose a book and have an adult read for 10 min. to you
or you can read for 10 min. to an adult

What did you read about today?
Draw a picture of what you read.

Writing and Spelling

Circle all the sight words from the word bank with a red crayon or pen.

Word Bank
the   of   and   a   to

1. The cat is fat.

2. He had many of them.

3. The cat and dog are friends.

4   I see a big jet.

5. We went to the park

Write the words from the word bank.

Trace and Color

TRICERATOPS

Day 20　　　　　Name_____

Bible

Have an adult read you a bible story from your
bible draw a picture of what you learned.

Math
Practice skip counting by 10's
Color the squares as you count have an adult help you.

Hundreds Chart

1	2	3	4	5	6	7	8	9	10
11	12	13	14	15	16	17	18	19	20
21	22	23	24	25	26	27	28	29	30
31	32	33	34	35	36	37	38	39	40
41	42	43	44	45	46	47	48	49	50
51	52	53	54	55	56	57	58	59	60
61	62	63	64	65	66	67	68	69	70
71	72	73	74	75	76	77	78	79	80
81	82	83	84	85	86	87	88	89	90
91	92	93	94	95	96	97	98	99	100

Reading

Choose a book and have an adult read for 10 min. to you
or you can read for 10 min. to an adult

What did you read about today?
Draw a picture of what you read.

Writing and Spelling
Circle all the sight words from the word bank with a red crayon or pen.

Word Bank

in   is   you   that   it

1.   The rat is in the tub.

2.   The cat is big.

3.   Can you see the fox?

4   That frog can jump.

5.   Can you help me dig it up?

Write the words from the word bank.

- - - - - - - - - - - - - - - - - - -

- - - - - - - - - - - - - - - - - - -

- - - - - - - - - - - - - - - - - - -

Trace and Color

T-REX

Day 21

Name_____

Bible
Have an adult read you a bible story from your bible draw a picture of what you learned.

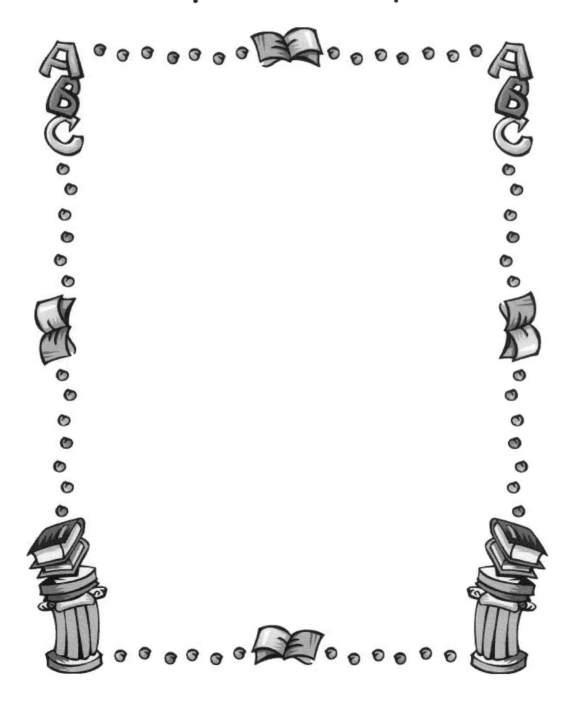

Math
Trace the numbers 1-100

Hundred Chart - Tracing

1	2	3	4	5	6	7	8	9	10
11	12	13	14	15	16	17	18	19	20
21	22	23	24	25	26	27	28	29	30
31	32	33	34	35	36	37	38	39	40
41	42	43	44	45	46	47	48	49	50
51	52	53	54	55	56	57	58	59	60
61	62	63	64	65	66	67	68	69	70
71	72	73	74	75	76	77	78	79	80
81	82	83	84	85	86	87	88	89	90
91	92	93	94	95	96	97	98	99	100

Reading

Choose a book and have an adult read for 10 min. to you
or you can read for 10 min. to an adult

What did you read about today?
Draw a picture of what you read.

Writing and Spelling
Circle all the sight words from the word bank with a red crayon or pen.

Word Bank

he   was   for   on   are

1.   He is my friend.

2.   The pig was big.

3.   The flower is for you.

4   The star is on the tree.

5.   The cat and dog are big.

Write the words from the word bank.

Trace and Color

STEGOSAURUS

Day 22   Name_____

Bible
Have an adult read you a bible story from your
bible draw a picture of what you learned.

Math
Trace the numbers 1-100

Hundred Chart - Tracing

1	2	3	4	5	6	7	8	9	10
11	12	13	14	15	16	17	18	19	20
21	22	23	24	25	26	27	28	29	30
31	32	33	34	35	36	37	38	39	40
41	42	43	44	45	46	47	48	49	50
51	52	53	54	55	56	57	58	59	60
61	62	63	64	65	66	67	68	69	70
71	72	73	74	75	76	77	78	79	80
81	82	83	84	85	86	87	88	89	90
91	92	93	94	95	96	97	98	99	100

Reading
Choose a book and have an adult read for 10 min. to you
or you can read for 10 min. to an adult

What did you read about today?
Draw a picture of what you read.

Writing and Spelling

Circle all the sight words from the word bank with a red crayon or pen.

Word Bank

as   with   his   they   I

---

1.   I am as big as an elephant.

2.   I like to play with my friends.

3.   His hat is red.

4   They both went with him.

5.   I like to ride the bus.

Write the words from the word bank.

- -

- -

- -

Trace and Color

BRACHIOSAURUS

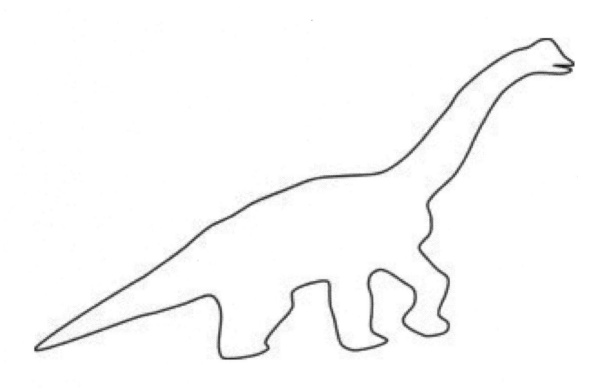

Day 23

Name_____

<u>Bible</u>
Have an adult read you a bible story from your
bible draw a picture of what you learned.

Math
Trace the numbers 1-100

Hundred Chart - Tracing

1	2	3	4	5	6	7	8	9	10
11	12	13	14	15	16	17	18	19	20
21	22	23	24	25	26	27	28	29	30
31	32	33	34	35	36	37	38	39	40
41	42	43	44	45	46	47	48	49	50
51	52	53	54	55	56	57	58	59	60
61	62	63	64	65	66	67	68	69	70
71	72	73	74	75	76	77	78	79	80
81	82	83	84	85	86	87	88	89	90
91	92	93	94	95	96	97	98	99	100

Reading

Choose a book and have an adult read for 10 min. to you
or you can read for 10 min. to an adult

What did you read about today?
Draw a picture of what you read.

Writing and Spelling

Circle all the sight words from the word bank with a red crayon or pen.

Word Bank

at   be   this   have   from

1.   The dog ran at me.

2.   Who will be the winner?

3.   This tree is tall.

4   I have a cold.

5.   I ride my bike home from school.

Write the words from the word bank.

- -

- -

- -

Trace and Color

CORYTHOSAURUS

Day 24   Name_____

Bible
Have an adult read you a bible story from your bible draw a picture of what you learned.

Math
Trace the numbers 1-100

Hundred Chart - Tracing

1	2	3	4	5	6	7	8	9	10
11	12	13	14	15	16	17	18	19	20
21	22	23	24	25	26	27	28	29	30
31	32	33	34	35	36	37	38	39	40
41	42	43	44	45	46	47	48	49	50
51	52	53	54	55	56	57	58	59	60
61	62	63	64	65	66	67	68	69	70
71	72	73	74	75	76	77	78	79	80
81	82	83	84	85	86	87	88	89	90
91	92	93	94	95	96	97	98	99	100

Reading

Choose a book and have an adult read for 10 min. to you
or you can read for 10 min. to an adult

What did you read about today?
Draw a picture of what you read.

Writing and Spelling

Circle all the sight words from the word bank with a red crayon or pen.

Word Bank

or   one   had   by   words

---

1.   Is this your shoe or mine?

2.   I had one cookie to eat.

3.   He had a blue coat.

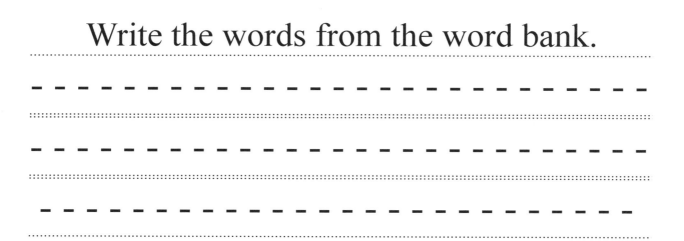

4   The frog sat by the pond.

5.   I know all my sight words.

Write the words from the word bank.

- - - - - - - - - - - - - - - - - - -

- - - - - - - - - - - - - - - - - - - -

- - - - - - - - - - - - - - - - - - - -

Be Creative Draw Something

Day 25   Name_____

<u>Bible</u>
Have an adult read you a bible story from your
bible draw a picture of what you learned.

Math
Trace the numbers 1-100

Hundred Chart - Tracing

1	2	3	4	5	6	7	8	9	10
11	12	13	14	15	16	17	18	19	20
21	22	23	24	25	26	27	28	29	30
31	32	33	34	35	36	37	38	39	40
41	42	43	44	45	46	47	48	49	50
51	52	53	54	55	56	57	58	59	60
61	62	63	64	65	66	67	68	69	70
71	72	73	74	75	76	77	78	79	80
81	82	83	84	85	86	87	88	89	90
91	92	93	94	95	96	97	98	99	100

<u>Reading</u>
Choose a book and have an adult read for 10 min. to you
or you can read for 10 min. to an adult

What did you read about today?
Draw a picture of what you read.

Writing and Spelling

Circle all the sight words from the word bank with a red crayon or pen.

Word Bank

but not what all were

1. A mouse is small but a fly is smaller.

2. I am not cold.

3. What is in the oven?

4 We all like to play games.

5. We were at the party.

Write the words from the word bank.

- -

- -

- -

Be Creative Draw Something

Day 26   Name_____

Bible
Have an adult read you a bible story from your bible draw a picture of what you learned.

Math
Fill in the missing numbers

Hundred Chart

1		3		5	6			9	10
	12	13			16	17			
21	22		24		26			29	
		33	34				38	39	
	42	43		45		47		49	
51			54			57	58		60
		63	64	65				69	70
	72		74		76		78		
81		83		85		87		89	
91		93	94			97	98		

Reading
Choose a book and have an adult read for 10 min. to you
or you can read for 10 min. to an adult

What did you read about today?
Draw a picture of what you read.

Writing and Spelling
Circle all the sight words from the word bank with a red crayon or pen.

Word Bank

there   use   an   each   which

1.   There is a small chick in the pen.

2.   I use a crayon to color.

3.   An ant bit me.

4   We each had a piece of cake.

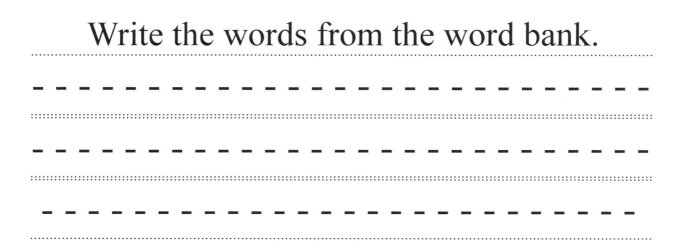

5.   Which toy should I choose?

Write the words from the word bank.

- - - - - - - - - - - - - - - - - - -

- - - - - - - - - - - - - - - - - - -

- - - - - - - - - - - - - - - - - - -

Draw My Habitat

Day 27   Name_____

Bible
Have an adult read you a bible story from your
bible draw a picture of what you learned.

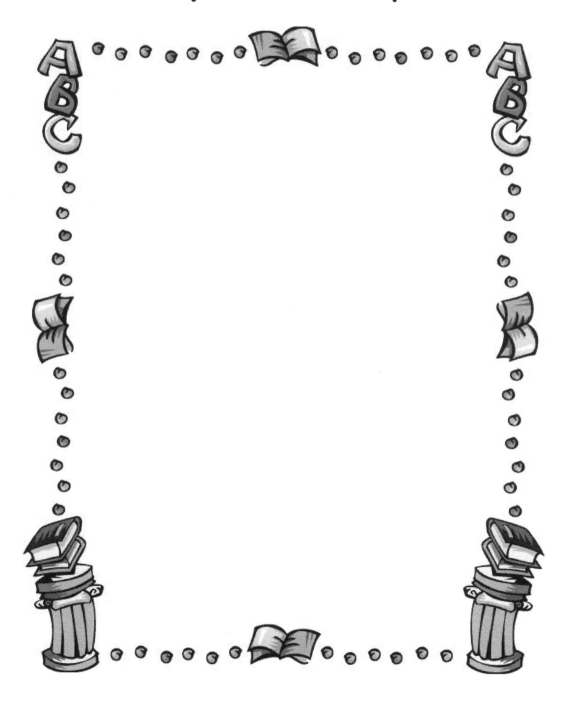

Math
Fill in the missing numbers

Hundred Chart

1		3		5	6			9	10
	12	13			16	17			
21	22		24		26			29	
		33	34				38	39	
	42	43		45		47		49	
51			54			57	58		60
		63	64	65				69	70
	72		74		76		78		
81		83		85		87		89	
91		93	94			97	98		

<u>Reading</u>
Choose a book and have an adult read for 10 min. to you
or you can read for 10 min. to an adult

What did you read about today?
Draw a picture of what you read.

Writing and Spelling

Circle all the sight words from the word bank with a red crayon or pen.

Word Bank

she   do   how   their   if

---

1. She is afraid of the dark.

2. How do I climb a tree?

3. Can you show me how to swim?

4 That is their ball.

5. I will be good if I can come with you.

Write the words from the word bank.

- - - - - - - - - - - - - - - - - - - -

- - - - - - - - - - - - - - - - - - - -

- - - - - - - - - - - - - - - - - - - -

Draw My Habitat

Day 28

Name_____

Bible

Have an adult read you a bible story from your
bible draw a picture of what you learned.

Math
Fill in the missing numbers

Hundred Chart

1		3		5	6			9	10
	12	13			16	17			
21	22		24		26			29	
		33	34				38	39	
	42	43		45		47		49	
51			54			57	58		60
		63	64	65				69	70
	72		74		76		78		
81		83		85		87		89	
91		93	94			97	98		

Reading
Choose a book and have an adult read for 10 min. to you or you can read for 10 min. to an adult

What did you read about today?
Draw a picture of what you read.

Writing and Spelling
Circle all the sight words from the word bank with a red crayon or pen.

Word Bank

will   up   other   about   out

1. I will read my book.

2. The balloon went up.

3. The other ball is better.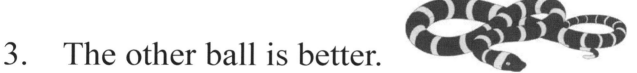

4 I learned all about bugs.

5. The snake got out of its cage.

Write the words from the word bank.

- -

- -

- -

Draw My Habitat

Day 29   Name_____

Bible

Have an adult read you a bible story from your
bible draw a picture of what you learned.

Math
Fill in the missing numbers

Hundred Chart

1		3		5	6			9	10
	12	13			16	17			
21	22		24		26			29	
		33	34				38	39	
	42	43		45		47		49	
51			54			57	58		60
		63	64	65				69	70
	72		74		76		78		
81		83		85		87		89	
91		93	94			97	98		

Reading

Choose a book and have an adult read for 10 min. to you
or you can read for 10 min. to an adult

What did you read about today?
Draw a picture of what you read.

Writing and Spelling
Circle all the sight words from the word bank with a red crayon or pen.

Word Bank

many   then   them   these   so

1.   I saw many ants.

2.   I went to bed then I woke up.

3.   Most of them went swimming.

4   These apples are good.

5.   It was so cold we went inside.

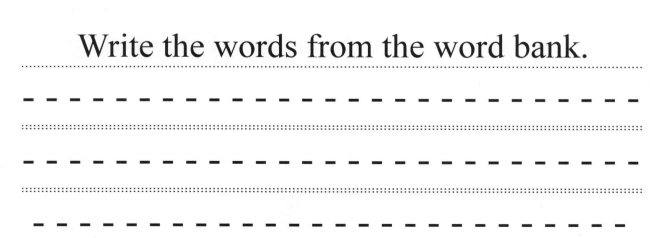

Write the words from the word bank.

Draw My Habitat

Day 30

Name_____

Bible
Have an adult read you a bible story from your bible draw a picture of what you learned.

Math
Fill in the missing numbers

Hundred Chart

1		3		5	6			9	10
	12	13			16	17			
21	22		24		26			29	
	33	34				38	39		
	42	43		45		47		49	
51			54			57	58		60
		63	64	65				69	70
	72		74		76		78		
81		83		85		87		89	
91		93	94			97	98		

<u>Reading</u>
Choose a book and have an adult read for 10 min. to you
or you can read for 10 min. to an adult

What did you read about today?
Draw a picture of what you read.

Writing and Spelling
Circle all the sight words from the word bank with a red crayon or pen.

Word Bank

some   her   would   make   like

1. I saw some dancers.

2. She scraped her knee.

3. I would like some pie.

4 My mom will make cookies.

5. I like to sing songs.

Write the words from the word bank.

Draw My Habitat

Day 31   Name_____

Bible

Have an adult read you a bible story from your bible draw a picture of what you learned.

Math
Fill in the missing numbers
1-100

Reading
Choose a book and have an adult read for 10 min. to you
or you can read for 10 min. to an adult

What did you read about today?
Draw a picture of what you read.

Writing and Spelling

Circle all the sight words from the word bank with a red crayon or pen.

Word Bank

him   into   time   has   look

---

1.   I saw him jump the fence.

2.   The bear went into its den.

3.   Is it time to go?

4   It has been so hot outside.

5.   Look at the stars.

Write the words from the word bank.

Draw My Habitat

Day 32   Name_____

Bible
Have an adult read you a bible story from your bible draw a picture of what you learned.

Math
Fill in the missing numbers
1-100

<u>Reading</u>
Choose a book and have an adult read for 10 min. to you
or you can read for 10 min. to an adult

What did you read about today?
Draw a picture of what you read.

Writing and Spelling

Circle all the sight words from the word bank with a red crayon or pen.

Word Bank

two   more   write   go   see

---

1.   I have two mittens.

2.   May I have more please?

3.   I need to write a letter.

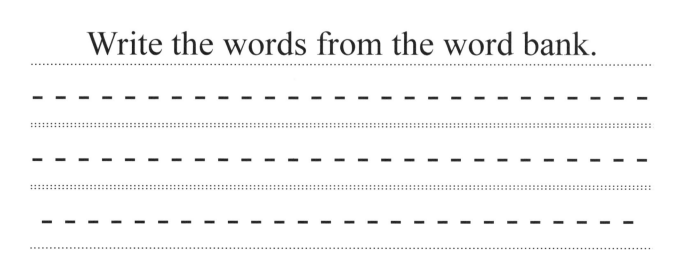

4   Lets go to the zoo.

5.   I see lots of flowers.

Write the words from the word bank.

Draw My Habitat

Day 33　　　　Name_____

Bible

Have an adult read you a bible story from your bible draw a picture of what you learned.

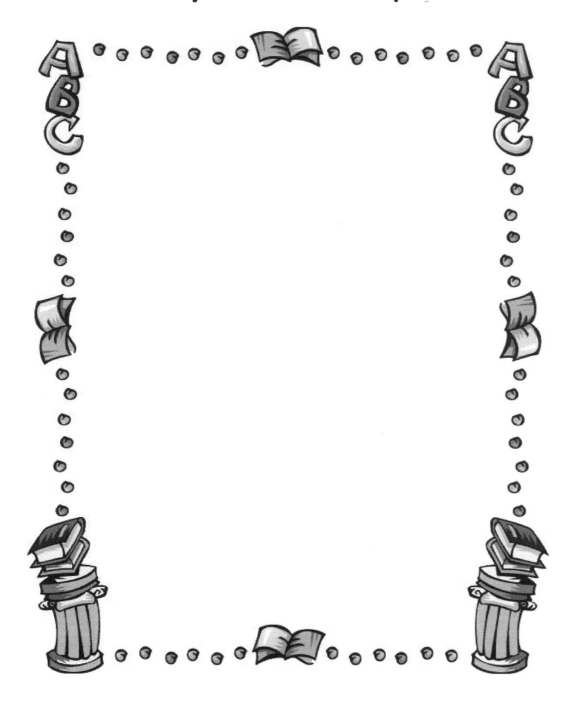

Math
Fill in the missing numbers
1-100

Reading

Choose a book and have an adult read for 10 min. to you
or you can read for 10 min. to an adult

What did you read about today?
Draw a picture of what you read.

Writing and Spelling
Circle all the sight words from the word bank with a red crayon or pen.

Word Bank

number   no   way   could   people

---

1.   My favorite number is 7.

2.   No, I don't want to play.

3.   I like the way you run.

4   Could you come over tomorrow?

5.   There are lots of people at the park today.

Write the words from the word bank.

- -

- -

- -

What Am I ?

_____

Write one fact about this animal.

_____

_____

Day 34   Name_____

Bible
Have an adult read you a bible story from your
bible draw a picture of what you learned.

Math
Fill in the missing numbers
1-100

<u>Reading</u>
Choose a book and have an adult read for 10 min. to you or you can read for 10 min. to an adult

What did you read about today?
Draw a picture of what you read.

Writing and Spelling
Circle all the sight words from the word bank with a red crayon or pen.

Word Bank

my   than   first   water   been

1. My cat is furry.

2. I am taller than he is.

3. I lost my first tooth.

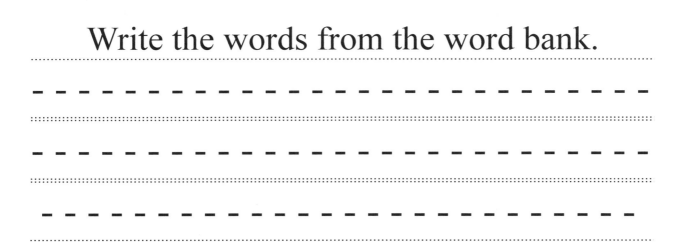

4   The bath water is just right.

5. I have been there before.

Write the words from the word bank.

- -

- -

- -

What Am I ?

_____

Write one fact about this animal.

_____

_____

Day 35

Name_____

Bible
Have an adult read you a bible story from your bible draw a picture of what you learned.

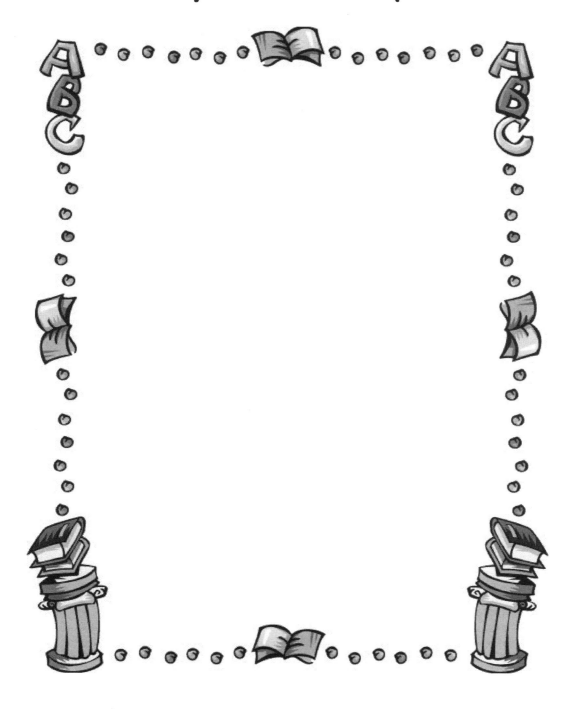

Math
Fill in the missing numbers
1-100

Reading
Choose a book and have an adult read for 10 min. to you
or you can read for 10 min. to an adult

What did you read about today?
Draw a picture of what you read.

Writing and Spelling

Circle all the sight words from the word bank with a red crayon or pen.

Word Bank

called   who   am   its   now

1. I called my dog and he came.

2. Who was at the door?

3. I am eight years old.

4   My dad said its to cold to swim.

5. My puppy is now a big dog.

Write the words from the word bank.

What Am I ?

_____

Write one fact about this animal.

_____

_____

Day 36
Name_____

Bible
Have an adult read you a bible story from your bible draw a picture of what you learned.

Math
Draw a line to match the domino with the number

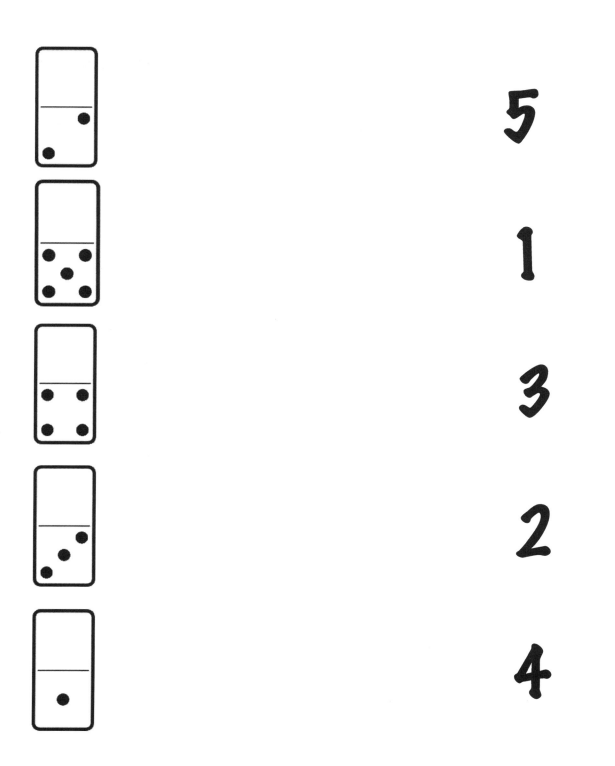

5

1

3

2

4

Reading
Choose a book and have an adult read for 10 min. to you or you can read for 10 min. to an adult

What did you read about today?
Draw a picture of what you read.

Writing and Spelling

practice writing your full name

First Name:

_____

-- -- -- -- -- -- -- -- -- -- -- -- -- -- -- --

_____

Middle Name:

_____

-- -- -- -- -- -- -- -- -- -- -- -- -- -- -- --

_____

Last Name:

_____

-- -- -- -- -- -- -- -- -- -- -- -- -- -- -- --

_____

Finish the Picture

What Am I ?

_____

Write one fact about this animal.

_____

_____

Day 37   Name_____

Bible

Have an adult read you a bible story from your bible draw a picture of what you learned.

Math
Draw a line to match the domino with the number

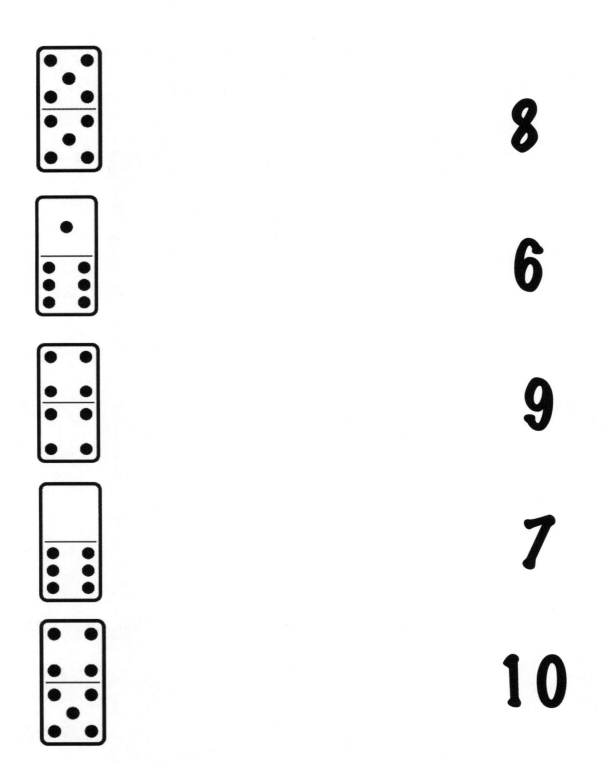

8

6

9

7

10

Reading
Choose a book and have an adult read for 10 min. to you
or you can read for 10 min. to an adult

What did you read about today?
Draw a picture of what you read.

Writing and Spelling

practice writing your full name

First Name:
_____

- -
_____

Middle Name:
_____

- -
_____

Last Name:
_____

- -
_____

Finish the Picture

What Am I ?

_____

Write one fact about this animal.

_____

_____

Day 38   Name_____

Bible
Have an adult read you a bible story from your
bible draw a picture of what you learned.

Math
Count How Many and write the number

<u>Reading</u>
Choose a book and have an adult read for 10 min. to you or you can read for 10 min. to an adult

What did you read about today?
Draw a picture of what you read.

Writing and Spelling

practice writing your full name

First Name:

- -

Middle Name:

- -

Last Name:

- -

Finish the Picture

What Am I ?

_____

Write one fact about this animal.

_____

_____

Day 39   Name_____

Bible

Have an adult read you a bible story from your
bible draw a picture of what you learned.

Math
Count How Many and write the number

_____

_____

_____

_____

Reading

Choose a book and have an adult read for 10 min. to you
or you can read for 10 min. to an adult

What did you read about today?
Draw a picture of what you read.

Writing and Spelling

practice writing your full name

First Name:
_____

Middle Name:
_____

Last Name:
_____

Finish the Picture

What Am I ?

_____

Write one fact about this animal.

_____

_____

Day 40　　　　　Name_____

Bible

Have an adult read you a bible story from your
bible draw a picture of what you learned.

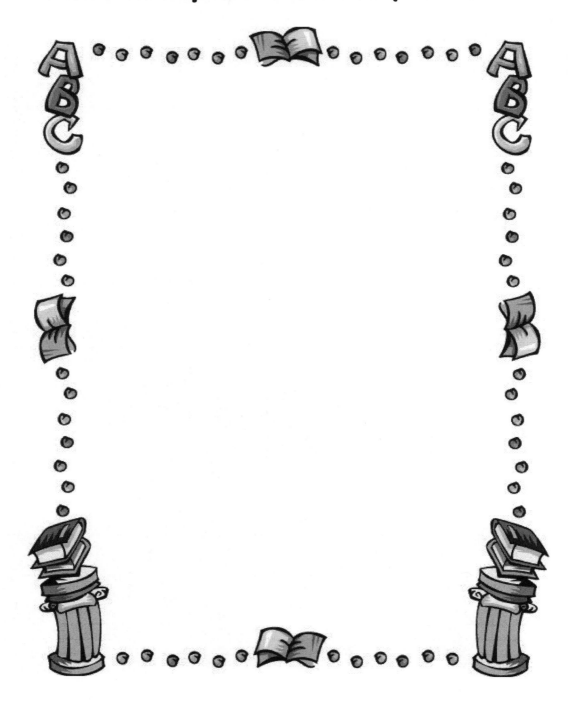

Math
color the number and trace the number word

One

Write the number word

_____

<u>Reading</u>
Choose a book and have an adult read for 10 min. to you
or you can read for 10 min. to an adult

What did you read about today?
Draw a picture of what you read.

Writing and Spelling

practice writing your full name

First Name:

‾‾

– –

Middle Name:

‾‾

– –

Last Name:

‾‾

– –

Finish the Picture

What Am I ?

_____

Write one fact about this animal.

_____

_____

Day 41   Name_____

Bible
Have an adult read you a bible story from your
bible draw a picture of what you learned.

Math
color the number and trace the number word

Write the number word

_____

- -

_____

Reading
Choose a book and have an adult read for 10 min. to you
or you can read for 10 min. to an adult

What did you read about today?
Draw a picture of what you read.

Writing and Spelling

practice writing your address

Address:
_____
- -
_____

City:
_____
- -
_____

State / Zip Code:
_____
- -
_____

Draw A Picture

What Am I ?

_____

Write one fact about this animal.

_____

_____

Day 42   Name_____

Bible

Have an adult read you a bible story from your
bible draw a picture of what you learned.

Math
color the number and trace the number word

three

Write the number word
_____

Reading
Choose a book and have an adult read for 10 min. to you or you can read for 10 min. to an adult

What did you read about today?
Draw a picture of what you read.

Writing and Spelling

practice writing your address

Address:
_____
– –
_____

City:
_____
– –
_____

State / Zip Code:
_____
– –
_____

Draw A Picture

What Am I ?

_____

Write one fact about this animal.

_____

_____

Day 43   Name_____

Bible
Have an adult read you a bible story from your
bible draw a picture of what you learned.

Math
color the number and trace the number word

four

Write the number word

_____

- -

_____

Reading
Choose a book and have an adult read for 10 min. to you
or you can read for 10 min. to an adult

What did you read about today?
Draw a picture of what you read.

Writing and Spelling

practice writing your address

Address:
_____

— — — — — — — — — — — — — — — — — —
_____

City:
_____

— — — — — — — — — — — — — — — — — —
_____

State / Zip Code:
_____

— — — — — — — — — — — — — — — — — —
_____

Draw A Picture

What Am I ?

_____

Write one fact about this animal.

_____

_____

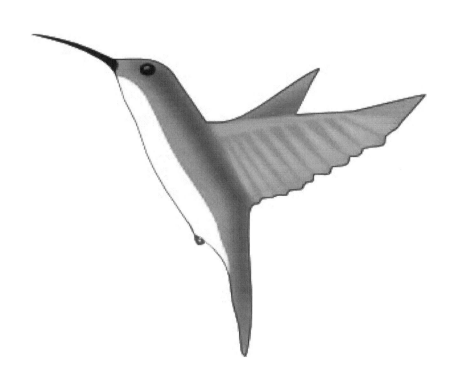

Day 44   Name_____

Bible

Have an adult read you a bible story from your bible draw a picture of what you learned.

Math
color the number and trace the number word

five

Write the number word
_____

_____

_____

Reading
Choose a book and have an adult read for 10 min. to you
or you can read for 10 min. to an adult

What did you read about today?
Draw a picture of what you read.

Writing and Spelling

practice writing your address

Address:
_____

- -

City:
_____

- -

State / Zip Code:
_____

- -

Draw A Picture

What Am I ?

_____

Write one fact about this animal.

_____

_____

Day 45   Name_____

Bible

Have an adult read you a bible story from your bible draw a picture of what you learned.

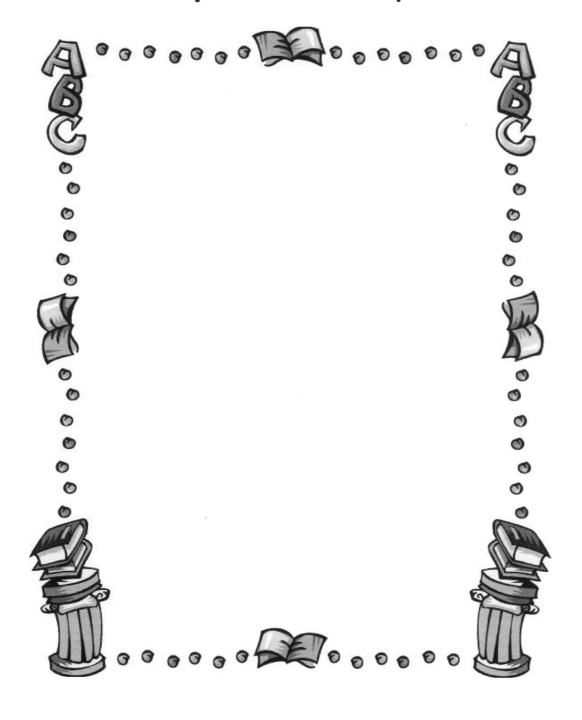

Math
color the number and trace the number word

Write the number word

_____

_____

Reading
Choose a book and have an adult read for 10 min. to you
or you can read for 10 min. to an adult

What did you read about today?
Draw a picture of what you read.

Writing and Spelling

practice writing your address

Address:
‾‾‾‾‾‾‾‾‾‾‾‾‾‾‾‾‾‾‾‾‾‾‾‾‾‾‾‾‾‾‾‾‾‾‾‾

- -

City:
‾‾‾‾‾‾‾‾‾‾‾‾‾‾‾‾‾‾‾‾‾‾‾‾‾‾‾‾‾‾‾‾‾‾‾‾

- -

State / Zip Code:
‾‾‾‾‾‾‾‾‾‾‾‾‾‾‾‾‾‾‾‾‾‾‾‾‾‾‾‾‾‾‾‾‾‾‾‾

- -

Draw A Picture

What Am I ?

_____

Write one fact about this animal.

_____

_____

Day 46   Name_____

Bible
Have an adult read you a bible story from your bible draw a picture of what you learned.

Math
color the number and trace the number word

seven

Write the number word

_____

- -

_____

Reading
Choose a book and have an adult read for 10 min. to you
or you can read for 10 min. to an adult

What did you read about today?
Draw a picture of what you read.

Writing and Spelling
Days of the week
Color the word then write it.

Sunday   _____

Monday   _____

Tuesday   _____

Wednesday   _____

Thursday   _____

Friday   _____

Saturday   _____

What Am I ?

_____

Write one fact about this animal.

_____

_____

Day 47

Name_____

Bible
Have an adult read you a bible story from your bible draw a picture of what you learned.

Math
color the number and trace the number word

eight

Write the number word

_____

- -

_____

Reading

Choose a book and have an adult read for 10 min. to you
or you can read for 10 min. to an adult

What did you read about today?
Draw a picture of what you read.

Writing and Spelling
Days of the week
Color the word then write it.

Sunday   _____

Monday   _____

Tuesday   _____

Wednesday   _____

Thursday   _____

Friday   _____

Saturday   _____

What Am I ?

_____

Write one fact about this animal.

_____

_____

Day 48   Name_____

Bible
Have an adult read you a bible story from your
bible draw a picture of what you learned.

Math
color the number and trace the number word

nine

Write the number word

_____

_ _

_____

Reading

Choose a book and have an adult read for 10 min. to you
or you can read for 10 min. to an adult

What did you read about today?
Draw a picture of what you read.

Writing and Spelling
Days of the week
Color the word then write it.

Sunday   _____

Monday   _____

Tuesday   _____

Wednesday   _____

Thursday   _____

Friday   _____

Saturday   _____

What Am I ?

_____

Write one fact about this animal.

_____

_____

Day 49   Name_____

<u>Bible</u>
Have an adult read you a bible story from your
bible draw a picture of what you learned.

Math
color the number and trace the number word

ten

Write the number word

_____

- -

_____

Reading
Choose a book and have an adult read for 10 min. to you or you can read for 10 min. to an adult

What did you read about today?
Draw a picture of what you read.

Writing and Spelling
Days of the week
Color the word then write it.

Sunday   _____

Monday   _____

Tuesday   _____

Wednesday   _____

Thursday   _____

Friday   _____

Saturday   _____

What Am I ?

_____

Write one fact about this animal.

_____

_____

Day 50   Name_____

Bible
Have an adult read you a bible story from your
bible draw a picture of what you learned.

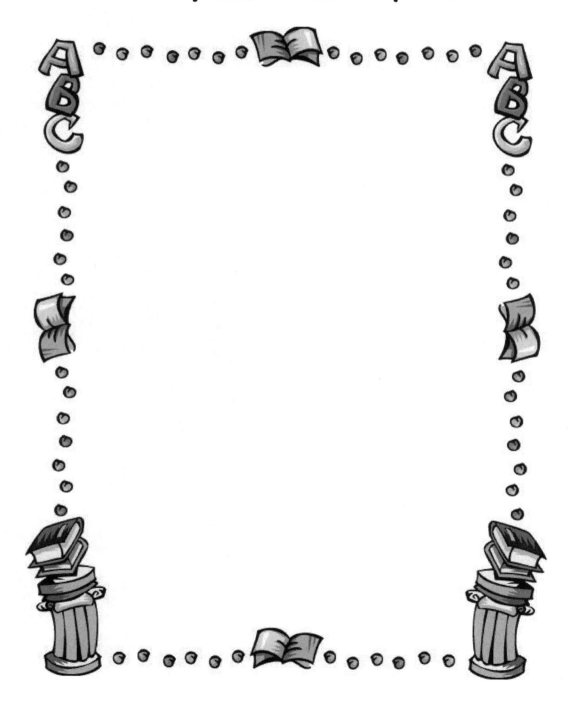

Math
Roll a pair of dice and add them up!

___ + ___ =

___ + ___ =

___ + ___ =

___ + ___ =

___ + ___ =

___ + ___ =

<u>Reading</u>
Choose a book and have an adult read for 10 min. to you
or you can read for 10 min. to an adult

What did you read about today?
Draw a picture of what you read.

Writing and Spelling
Days of the week
Color the word then write it.

Sunday   _____

Monday   _____

Tuesday   _____

Wednesday   _____

Thursday   _____

Friday   _____

Saturday   _____

What Am I ?

_____

Write one fact about this animal.

_____

_____

Day 51

Name_____

Bible
Have an adult read you a bible story from your bible draw a picture of what you learned.

Math
Roll a pair of dice and add them up!

___ + ___ =

___ + ___ =

___ + ___ =

___ + ___ =

___ + ___ =

___ + ___ =

Reading

Choose a book and have an adult read for 10 min. to you
or you can read for 10 min. to an adult

What did you read about today?
Draw a picture of what you read.

Writing and Spelling
Days of the week
Color the word then write it.

Sunday   _____

Monday   _____

Tuesday   _____

Wednesday   _____

Thursday   _____

Friday   _____

Saturday   _____

What Am I ?

_____

Write one fact about this animal.

_____

_____

Day 52   Name_____

<u>Bible</u>
Have an adult read you a bible story from your
bible draw a picture of what you learned.

Math
Roll a pair of dice and add them up!

____+____=

____+____=

____+____=

____+____=

____+____=

____+____=

Reading

Choose a book and have an adult read for 10 min. to you
or you can read for 10 min. to an adult

What did you read about today?
Draw a picture of what you read.

Writing and Spelling
Days of the week
Color the word then write it.

Sunday   _____

Monday   _____

Tuesday   _____

Wednesday   _____

Thursday   _____

Friday   _____

Saturday   _____

What Am I ?

_____

Write one fact about this animal.

_____

_____

Day 53   Name_____

Bible
Have an adult read you a bible story from your bible draw a picture of what you learned.

Math
Roll a pair of dice and add them up!

____ + ____ =

____ + ____ =

____ + ____ =

____ + ____ =

____ + ____ =

____ + ____ =

Reading

Choose a book and have an adult read for 10 min. to you
or you can read for 10 min. to an adult

What did you read about today?
Draw a picture of what you read.

Writing and Spelling
Days of the week
Color the word then write it.

Sunday   _____

Monday   _____

Tuesday   _____

Wednesday   _____

Thursday   _____

Friday   _____

Saturday   _____

What Am I ?

_____

Write one fact about this animal.

_____

_____

Day 54   Name_____

Bible

Have an adult read you a bible story from your
bible draw a picture of what you learned.

Math
Roll a pair of dice and add them up!

___ + ___ =

___ + ___ =

___ + ___ =

___ + ___ =

___ + ___ =

___ + ___ =

Reading
Choose a book and have an adult read for 10 min. to you
or you can read for 10 min. to an adult

What did you read about today?
Draw a picture of what you read.

Writing and Spelling
Days of the week
Color the word then write it.

Sunday   _____

Monday   _____

Tuesday   _____

Wednesday   _____

Thursday   _____

Friday   _____

Saturday   _____

What Am I ?

_____

Write one fact about this animal.

_____

_____

Day 55   Name_____

Bible

Have an adult read you a bible story from your bible draw a picture of what you learned.

Math
Roll a pair of dice and add them up!

___+___=

___+___=

___+___=

___+___=

___+___=

___+___=

Reading

Choose a book and have an adult read for 10 min. to you
or you can read for 10 min. to an adult

What did you read about today?
Draw a picture of what you read.

Writing and Spelling
Days of the week
Color the word then write it.

Sunday   _____

Monday   _____

Tuesday   _____

Wednesday   _____

Thursday   _____

Friday   _____

Saturday   _____

What Am I ?

_____

Write one fact about this animal.

_____

_____

Day 56   Name_____

<u>Bible</u>
Have an adult read you a bible story from your
bible draw a picture of what you learned.

Math
Roll a pair of dice and add them up!

___+___=

___+___=

___+___=

___+___=

___+___=

___+___=

Reading
Choose a book and have an adult read for 10 min. to you
or you can read for 10 min. to an adult

What did you read about today?
Draw a picture of what you read.

Writing and Spelling
Months of the year
Color the word then write it.

January   _____

February   _____

March   _____

April   _____

May   _____

June   _____

July   _____

Lets Learn the Planets!
Mercury

Mercury is the closest planet to the Sun and the first planet in our solar system.

Day 57   Name_____

<u>Bible</u>
Have an adult read you a bible story from your
bible draw a picture of what you learned.

Math
Roll a pair of dice and add them up!

___ + ___ =

___ + ___ =

___ + ___ =

___ + ___ =

___ + ___ =

___ + ___ =

Reading
Choose a book and have an adult read for 10 min. to you or you can read for 10 min. to an adult

What did you read about today?
Draw a picture of what you read.

Writing and Spelling
Months of the year
Color the word then write it.

August   _____

September   _____

October   _____

November   _____

December   _____

Lets Learn the Planets!
Venus

Venus is second planet in our solar system.

Day 58   Name_____

Bible
Have an adult read you a bible story from your bible draw a picture of what you learned.

Math
Roll a pair of dice and add them up!

___ + ___ =

___ + ___ =

___ + ___ =

___ + ___ =

___ + ___ =

___ + ___ =

Reading
Choose a book and have an adult read for 10 min. to you
or you can read for 10 min. to an adult

What did you read about today?
Draw a picture of what you read.

Writing and Spelling
Months of the year
Color the word then write it.

January   _____

February   _____

March   _____

April   _____

May   _____

June   _____

July   _____

Lets Learn the Planets!
Earth

Earth is third planet in our solar system.

Day 59　　　　Name_____

Bible
Have an adult read you a bible story from your
bible draw a picture of what you learned.

Math
Roll a pair of dice and add them up!

___+___=

___+___=

___+___=

___+___=

___+___=

___+___=

Reading
Choose a book and have an adult read for 10 min. to you
or you can read for 10 min. to an adult

What did you read about today?
Draw a picture of what you read.

Writing and Spelling
Months of the year
Color the word then write it.

August _____

September _____

October _____

November _____

December _____

Lets Learn the Planets!
Mars

Mars is fourth planet in our solar system.

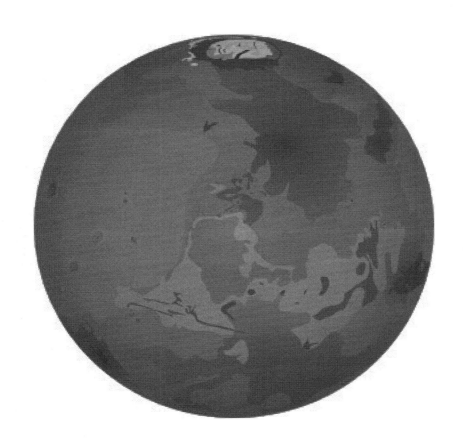

Day 60   Name_____

Bible
Have an adult read you a bible story from your bible draw a picture of what you learned.

Math
Roll a pair of dice and add them up!

___+___=

___+___=

___+___=

___+___=

___+___=

___+___=

Reading
Choose a book and have an adult read for 10 min. to you
or you can read for 10 min. to an adult

What did you read about today?
Draw a picture of what you read.

Writing and Spelling
Months of the year
Color the word then write it.

January _____

February _____

March _____

April _____

May _____

June _____

July _____

Lets Learn the Planets!
Jupiter

Jupiter is fifth planet in our solar system.

Day 61   Name_____

Bible
Have an adult read you a bible story from your
bible draw a picture of what you learned.

Math
Roll a pair of dice and add them up!

___+___=

___+___=

___+___=

___+___=

___+___=

___+___=

Reading

Choose a book and have an adult read for 10 min. to you
or you can read for 10 min. to an adult

What did you read about today?
Draw a picture of what you read.

Writing and Spelling
Months of the year
Color the word then write it.

August   _____

September   _____

October   _____

November   _____

December   _____

Lets Learn the Planets!
Saturn

Saturn is the sixth planet in our solar system.

Day 62   Name_____

Bible
Have an adult read you a bible story from your
bible draw a picture of what you learned.

Math
Roll a pair of dice and add them up!

___+___=

___+___=

___+___=

___+___=

___+___=

___+___=

<u>Reading</u>
Choose a book and have an adult read for 10 min. to you
or you can read for 10 min. to an adult

What did you read about today?
Draw a picture of what you read.

Writing and Spelling
Months of the year
Color the word then write it.

January   _____

February   _____

March   _____

April   _____

May   _____

June   _____

July   _____

Lets Learn the Planets!
Uranus

Uranus is the seventh planet in our solar system.

Day 63   Name_____

Bible
Have an adult read you a bible story from your
bible draw a picture of what you learned.

Math
Roll a pair of dice and add them up!

___+___=

___+___=

___+___=

___+___=

___+___=

___+___=

Reading
Choose a book and have an adult read for 10 min. to you or you can read for 10 min. to an adult

What did you read about today?
Draw a picture of what you read.

Writing and Spelling
Months of the year
Color the word then write it.

August _____

September _____

October _____

November _____

December _____

Lets Learn the Planets!
Neptune

Neptune is the eighth planet in our solar system.

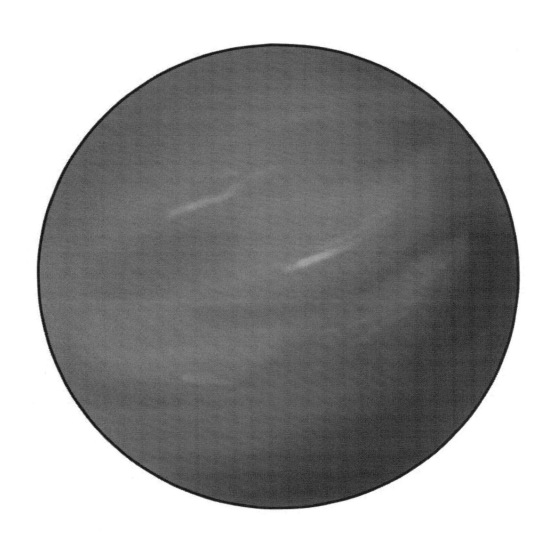

Day 64   Name_____

Bible
Have an adult read you a bible story from your bible draw a picture of what you learned.

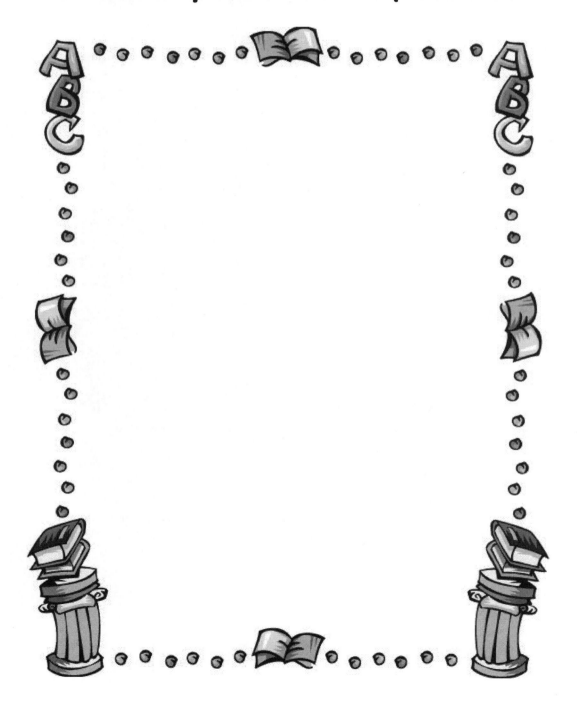

Math
Roll a pair of dice and add them up!

____+____=

____+____=

____+____=

____+____=

____+____=

____+____=

Reading
Choose a book and have an adult read for 10 min. to you
or you can read for 10 min. to an adult

What did you read about today?
Draw a picture of what you read.

Writing and Spelling
Months of the year
Color the word then write it.

January   _____

February   _____

March   _____

April   _____

May   _____

June   _____

July   _____

Lets Learn the Planets!
Pluto

Pluto is the ninth planet in our solar system.

Day 65   Name_____

Bible

Have an adult read you a bible story from your bible draw a picture of what you learned.

Math
Roll a pair of dice and add them up!

___+___=

___+___=

___+___=

___+___=

___+___=

___+___=

<u>Reading</u>
Choose a book and have an adult read for 10 min. to you
or you can read for 10 min. to an adult

What did you read about today?
Draw a picture of what you read.

Writing and Spelling
Months of the year
Color the word then write it.

August   _____

September   _____

October   _____

November   _____

December   _____

Lets review the planets!

Here is a very easy way to remember the planets in order. Memorize this phrase.

Color the Picture

Mercury... My
Venus...Very
Earth... Eager
Mars.. Mother
Jupiter... Just
Saturn... Served
Uranus... Us
Neptune... Nine
Pluto... Pizzas

Mercury

Venus

Earth

Mars

Jupiter

Saturn

Uranus

Neptune

Pluto

Day 66   Name_____

Bible
Have an adult read you a bible story from your
bible draw a picture of what you learned.

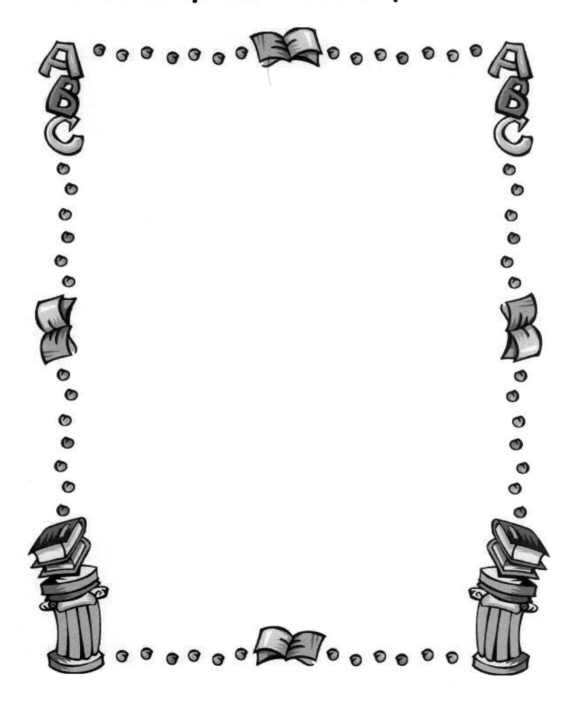

Math
Roll a pair of dice and add them up!

____+____=

____+____=

____+____=

____+____=

____+____=

____+____=

Reading
Choose a book and have an adult read for 10 min. to you
or you can read for 10 min. to an adult

What did you read about today?
Draw a picture of what you read.

Writing and Spelling
Look at the picture and write a story about it. Have an adult help you.

_____

_____

_____

_____

_____

_____

_____

_____

Lets review the planets!

What is the first planet in our solar system?

_____

_____

_____

Draw a picture of the planet

Day 67   Name_____

Bible

Have an adult read you a bible story from your bible draw a picture of what you learned.

Math
Roll a pair of dice and add them up!

_____ + _____ =

_____ + _____ =

_____ + _____ =

_____ + _____ =

_____ + _____ =

_____ + _____ =

Reading
Choose a book and have an adult read for 10 min. to you
or you can read for 10 min. to an adult

What did you read about today?
Draw a picture of what you read.

Writing and Spelling
Look at the picture and write a story about it. Have an adult help you.

_____

_____

_____

_____

_____

_____

_____

_____

Lets review the planets!

What is the second planet in our solar system?

_____

- -

_____

Draw a picture of the planet

Day 68   Name_____

Bible
Have an adult read you a bible story from your bible draw a picture of what you learned.

Math
Roll a pair of dice and add them up!

____+____=

____+____=

____+____=

____+____=

____+____=

____+____=

Reading
Choose a book and have an adult read for 10 min. to you
or you can read for 10 min. to an adult

What did you read about today?
Draw a picture of what you read.

Writing and Spelling
Look at the picture and write a story about it. Have an adult help you.

_____

_____

_____

_____

_____

_____

_____

Lets review the planets!

What is the third planet in our solar system?

_____

_____

_____

Draw a picture of the planet

Day 69　　　Name_____

Bible
Have an adult read you a bible story from your
bible draw a picture of what you learned.

Math
Roll a pair of dice and add them up!

_____+_____=

_____+_____=

_____+_____=

_____+_____=

_____+_____=

_____+_____=

Reading
Choose a book and have an adult read for 10 min. to you or you can read for 10 min. to an adult

What did you read about today?
Draw a picture of what you read.

Writing and Spelling
Look at the picture and write a story about it. Have an adult help you.

_____

_____

_____

_____

_____

_____

_____

_____

Lets review the planets!

What is the fourth planet in our solar system?

_____

- -

_____

Draw a picture of the planet

Day 70   Name_____

Bible
Have an adult read you a bible story from your
bible draw a picture of what you learned.

Math
Roll a pair of dice and add them up!

_____+_____=

_____+_____=

_____+_____=

_____+_____=

_____+_____=

_____+_____=

Reading
Choose a book and have an adult read for 10 min. to you
or you can read for 10 min. to an adult

What did you read about today?
Draw a picture of what you read.

Writing and Spelling
Look at the picture and write a story about it. Have an adult help you.

_____

_____

_____

_____

_____

_____

_____

_____

Lets review the planets!

What is the fifth planet in our solar system?

_____

- -

_____

Draw a picture of the planet

Day 71   Name_____

Bible
Have an adult read you a bible story from your
bible draw a picture of what you learned.

Math
Roll a pair of dice and add them up!

_____ + _____ =

_____ + _____ =

_____ + _____ =

_____ + _____ =

_____ + _____ =

_____ + _____ =

Reading
Choose a book and have an adult read for 10 min. to you
or you can read for 10 min. to an adult

What did you read about today?
Draw a picture of what you read.

Writing and Spelling
Look at the picture and write a story about it. Have an adult help you.

_____

_____

_____

_____

_____

_____

_____

_____

Lets review the planets!

What is the sixth planet in our solar system?

_____

_____

Draw a picture of the planet

Day 72   Name_____

Bible
Have an adult read you a bible story from your
bible draw a picture of what you learned.

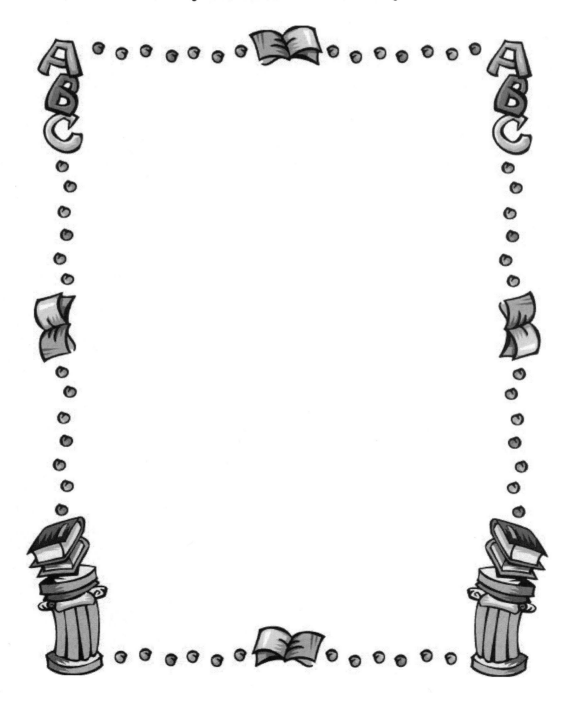

Math
Roll a pair of dice and add them up!

____+____=

____+____=

____+____=

____+____=

____+____=

____+____=

Reading
Choose a book and have an adult read for 10 min. to you
or you can read for 10 min. to an adult

What did you read about today?
Draw a picture of what you read.

Writing and Spelling
Look at the picture and write a story about it. Have an adult help you.

_____

_____

_____

_____

_____

_____

_____

_____

Lets review the planets!

What is the seventh planet in our solar system?

_____

- -

_____

Draw a picture of the planet

Day 73   Name_____

Bible
Have an adult read you a bible story from your
bible draw a picture of what you learned.

Math
Roll a pair of dice and add them up!

_____+_____=

_____+_____=

_____+_____=

_____+_____=

_____+_____=

_____+_____=

Reading
Choose a book and have an adult read for 10 min. to you
or you can read for 10 min. to an adult

What did you read about today?
Draw a picture of what you read.

Writing and Spelling
Look at the picture and write a story about it. Have an adult help you.

_____

_____

_____

_____

_____

_____

_____

_____

Lets review the planets!

What is the eighth planet in our solar system?

_____

― ―

_____

Draw a picture of the planet

Day 74   Name_____

Bible
Have an adult read you a bible story from your bible draw a picture of what you learned.

Math
Roll a pair of dice and add them up!

___ + ___ =

___ + ___ =

___ + ___ =

___ + ___ =

___ + ___ =

___ + ___ =

Reading
Choose a book and have an adult read for 10 min. to you
or you can read for 10 min. to an adult

What did you read about today?
Draw a picture of what you read.

Writing and Spelling

Look at the picture and write a story about it. Have an adult help you.

_____

_____

_____

_____

_____

_____

_____

Lets review the planets!

What is the ninth planet in our solar system?

_____

- -

_____

Draw a picture of the planet

Day 75　　　　　**Name**_____

Bible

Have an adult read you a bible story from your bible draw a picture of what you learned.

Math
Roll a pair of dice and add them up!

___+___=

___+___=

___+___=

___+___=

___+___=

___+___=

Reading
Choose a book and have an adult read for 10 min. to you
or you can read for 10 min. to an adult

What did you read about today?
Draw a picture of what you read.

Writing and Spelling
Look at the picture and write a story about it. Have an adult help you.

_____

_____

_____

_____

_____

_____

_____

_____

Lets review the planets!

Do you remember the rhyme to say the planets in order?

If so say it to an adult and draw the planets in order below.

Day 76   Name_____

Bible

Have an adult read you a bible story from your bible draw a picture of what you learned.

Math
Roll a pair of dice and add them up!

___ + ___ =

___ + ___ =

___ + ___ =

___ + ___ =

___ + ___ =

___ + ___ =

Reading

Choose a book and have an adult read for 10 min. to you
or you can read for 10 min. to an adult

What did you read about today?
Draw a picture of what you read.

Writing and Spelling
Lets learn Cursive

This is the alphabet in cursive these are capitol and lower case letters. Trace the letters, have and adult help you .

Aa Bb Cc Dd Ee Ff Gg

Hh Ii Jj Kk Ll Mm Nn

Oo Pp Qq Rr Ss Tt Uu Vv

Ww Xx Yy Zz

Lets review the planets!

Do you remember the rhyme to say the planets in order?

If so say it to an adult and draw the planets in order below.

Day 77　　　　Name_____

Bible
Have an adult read you a bible story from your
bible draw a picture of what you learned.

Math
Roll a pair of dice and add them up!

___+___=

___+___=

___+___=

___+___=

___+___=

___+___=

Reading

Choose a book and have an adult read for 10 min. to you
or you can read for 10 min. to an adult

What did you read about today?
Draw a picture of what you read.

Writing and Spelling
Lets learn Cursive

This is the alphabet in cursive these are capitol and lower case letters. Trace the letters, have and adult help you .

Aa Bb Cc Dd Ee Ff Gg

Hh Ii Jj Kk Ll Mm Nn

Oo Pp Qq Rr Ss Tt Uu Vv

Ww Xx Yy Zz

Nature Study

Find something in nature and draw it.

Day 78　　　　Name_____

Bible

Have an adult read you a bible story from your
bible draw a picture of what you learned.

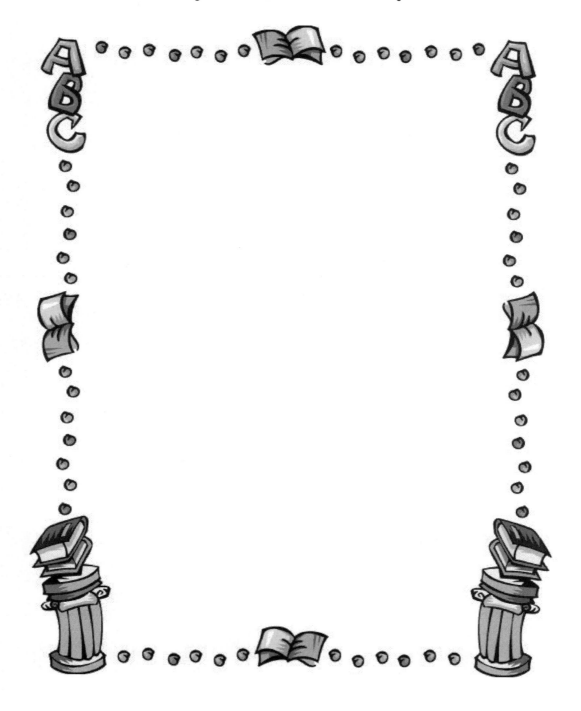

Math
Roll a pair of dice and add them up!

___ + ___ =

___ + ___ =

___ + ___ =

___ + ___ =

___ + ___ =

___ + ___ =

Reading
Choose a book and have an adult read for 10 min. to you
or you can read for 10 min. to an adult

What did you read about today?
Draw a picture of what you read.

Writing and Spelling
Lets learn Cursive

This is the alphabet in cursive these are capitol and lower case letters. Trace the letters, have and adult help you .

Aa Bb Cc Dd Ee Ff Gg

Hh Ii Jj Kk Ll Mm Nn

Oo Pp Qq Rr Ss Tt Uu Vv

Ww Xx Yy Zz

Nature Study
Find something in nature and draw it.

Day 79   Name_____

Bible
Have an adult read you a bible story from your
bible draw a picture of what you learned.

Math
Roll a pair of dice and add them up!

____+____=

____+____=

____+____=

____+____=

____+____=

____+____=

Reading
Choose a book and have an adult read for 10 min. to you
or you can read for 10 min. to an adult

What did you read about today?
Draw a picture of what you read.

Writing and Spelling
Lets learn Cursive

This is the alphabet in cursive these are capitol and lower case letters. Trace the letters, have and adult help you .

Aa Bb Cc Dd Ee Ff Gg

Hh Ii Jj Kk Ll Mm Nn

Oo Pp Qq Rr Ss Tt Uu Vv

Ww Xx Yy Zz

Nature Study
Find something in nature and draw it.

Day 80   Name_____

Bible
Have an adult read you a bible story from your
bible draw a picture of what you learned.

Math
Roll a pair of dice and add them up!

____+____=

____+____=

____+____=

____+____=

____+____=

____+____=

Reading

Choose a book and have an adult read for 10 min. to you
or you can read for 10 min. to an adult

What did you read about today?
Draw a picture of what you read.

Writing and Spelling
Lets learn Cursive

This is the alphabet in cursive these are capitol and lower case letters. Trace the letters, have and adult help you .

Aa Bb Cc Dd Ee Ff Gg

Hh Ii Jj Kk Ll Mm Nn

Oo Pp Qq Rr Ss Tt Uu Vv

Ww Xx Yy Zz

Nature Study
Find something in nature and draw it.

Day 81   Name_____

Bible
Have an adult read you a bible story from your bible draw a picture of what you learned.

Math
Roll a pair of dice and add them up!

___+___=

___+___=

___+___=

___+___=

___+___=

___+___=

Reading
Choose a book and have an adult read for 10 min. to you
or you can read for 10 min. to an adult

What did you read about today?
Draw a picture of what you read.

Writing and Spelling
Lets learn Cursive

This is the alphabet in cursive these are capitol and lower case letters. Trace the letters, have and adult help you.

Aa Bb Cc Dd Ee Ff Gg

Hh Ii Jj Kk Ll Mm Nn

Oo Pp Qq Rr Ss Tt Uu Vv

Ww Xx Yy Zz

Nature Study
Find something in nature and draw it.

Day 82   Name_____

Bible

Have an adult read you a bible story from your bible draw a picture of what you learned.

Math
Roll a pair of dice and add them up!

___ + ___ =

___ + ___ =

___ + ___ =

___ + ___ =

___ + ___ =

___ + ___ =

Reading
Choose a book and have an adult read for 10 min. to you
or you can read for 10 min. to an adult

What did you read about today?
Draw a picture of what you read.

Writing and Spelling
Lets learn Cursive

This is the alphabet in cursive these are capitol and lower case letters. Trace the letters, have and adult help you .

Aa Bb Cc Dd Ee Ff Gg

Hh Ii Jj Kk Ll Mm Nn

Oo Pp Qq Rr Ss Tt Uu Vv

Ww Xx Yy Zz

Nature Study
Find something in nature and draw it.

Day 83   Name_____

Bible

Have an adult read you a bible story from your
bible draw a picture of what you learned.

Math
Roll a pair of dice and add them up!

____+____=

____+____=

____+____=

____+____=

____+____=

____+____=

Reading
Choose a book and have an adult read for 10 min. to you
or you can read for 10 min. to an adult

What did you read about today?
Draw a picture of what you read.

Writing and Spelling
Lets learn Cursive

This is the alphabet in cursive these are capitol and lower case letters. Trace the letters, have and adult help you .

Aa Bb Cc Dd Ee Ff Gg

Hh Ii Jj Kk Ll Mm Nn

Oo Pp Qq Rr Ss Tt Uu Vv

Ww Xx Yy Zz

Nature Study
Find something in nature and draw it.

Day 84   Name_____

Bible
Have an adult read you a bible story from your bible draw a picture of what you learned.

Math
Roll a pair of dice and add them up!

____ + ____ =

____ + ____ =

____ + ____ =

____ + ____ =

____ + ____ =

____ + ____ =

Reading
Choose a book and have an adult read for 10 min. to you
or you can read for 10 min. to an adult

What did you read about today?
Draw a picture of what you read.

Writing and Spelling
Lets learn Cursive

This is the alphabet in cursive these are capitol and lower case letters. Trace the letters, have and adult help you .

Aa Bb Cc Dd Ee Ff Gg

Hh Ii Jj Kk Ll Mm Nn

Oo Pp Qq Rr Ss Tt Uu Vv

Ww Xx Yy Zz

Nature Study
Find something in nature and draw it.

Day 85 Name_____

Bible

Have an adult read you a bible story from your bible draw a picture of what you learned.

Math
Roll a pair of dice and add them up!

___ + ___ =

___ + ___ =

___ + ___ =

___ + ___ =

___ + ___ =

___ + ___ =

Reading
Choose a book and have an adult read for 10 min. to you
or you can read for 10 min. to an adult

What did you read about today?
Draw a picture of what you read.

Writing and Spelling
Lets learn Cursive

This is the alphabet in cursive these are capitol and lower case letters. Trace the letters, have and adult help you

Aa Bb Cc Dd Ee Ff Gg

Hh Ii Jj Kk Ll Mm Nn

Oo Pp Qq Rr Ss Tt Uu Vv

Ww Xx Yy Zz

Nature Study
Find something in nature and draw it.

Day 86   Name_____

Bible
Have an adult read you a bible story from your bible draw a picture of what you learned.

Math
Roll a pair of dice and add them up!

____ + ____ =

____ + ____ =

____ + ____ =

____ + ____ =

____ + ____ =

____ + ____ =

<u>Reading</u>
Choose a book and have an adult read for 10 min. to you
or you can read for 10 min. to an adult

What did you read about today?
Draw a picture of what you read.

Writing and Spelling
Lets learn Cursive

This is the alphabet in cursive these are capitol and lower case letters. Trace the letters, have and adult help you

Aa Bb Cc Dd Ee Ff Gg

Hh Ii Jj Kk Ll Mm Nn

Oo Pp Qq Rr Ss Tt Uu Vv

Ww Xx Yy Zz

Nature Study
Find something in nature and draw it.

Day 87   Name_____

Bible

Have an adult read you a bible story from your bible draw a picture of what you learned.

Math
Roll a pair of dice and add them up!

____+____=

____+____=

____+____=

____+____=

____+____=

____+____=

Reading
Choose a book and have an adult read for 10 min. to you
or you can read for 10 min. to an adult

What did you read about today?
Draw a picture of what you read.

Writing and Spelling
Lets learn Cursive

This is the alphabet in cursive these are capitol and lower case letters. Trace the letters, have and adult help you

Aa Bb Cc Dd Ee Ff Gg

Hh Ii Jj Kk Ll Mm Nn

Oo Pp Qq Rr Ss Tt Uu Vv

Ww Xx Yy Zz

Nature Study
Find something in nature and draw it.

Day 88   Name_____

Bible
Have an adult read you a bible story from your bible draw a picture of what you learned.

Math
Roll a pair of dice and add them up!

____+____=

____+____=

____+____=

____+____=

____+____=

____+____=

Reading
Choose a book and have an adult read for 10 min. to you
or you can read for 10 min. to an adult

What did you read about today?
Draw a picture of what you read.

Writing and Spelling
Lets learn Cursive

This is the alphabet in cursive these are capitol and lower case letters. Trace the letters, have and adult help you

Aa Bb Cc Dd Ee Ff Gg

Hh Ii Jj Kk Ll Mm Nn

Oo Pp Qq Rr Ss Tt Uu Vv

Ww Xx Yy Zz

Nature Study
Find something in nature and draw it.

Day 89   Name_____

Bible
Have an adult read you a bible story from your bible draw a picture of what you learned.

Math
Roll a pair of dice and add them up!

____+____=

____+____=

____+____=

____+____=

____+____=

____+____=

<u>Reading</u>
Choose a book and have an adult read for 10 min. to you
or you can read for 10 min. to an adult

What did you read about today?
Draw a picture of what you read.

Writing and Spelling
Lets learn Cursive

This is the alphabet in cursive these are capitol and lower case letters. Trace the letters, have and adult help you

Aa Bb Cc Dd Ee Ff Gg

Hh Ii Jj Kk Ll Mm Nn

Oo Pp Qq Rr Ss Tt Uu Vv

Ww Xx Yy Zz

Nature Study
Find something in nature and draw it.

Day 90   Name_____

Bible

Have an adult read you a bible story from your bible draw a picture of what you learned.

Math
Roll a pair of dice and add them up!

___+___=

___+___=

___+___=

___+___=

___+___=

___+___=

Reading
Choose a book and have an adult read for 10 min. to you
or you can read for 10 min. to an adult

What did you read about today?
Draw a picture of what you read.

Writing and Spelling
Lets learn Cursive

This is the alphabet in cursive these are capitol and lower case letters. Trace the letters, have and adult help you

Aa Bb Cc Dd Ee Ff Gg

Hh Ii Jj Kk Ll Mm Nn

Oo Pp Qq Rr Ss Tt Uu Vv

Ww Xx Yy Zz

Nature Study
Find something in nature and draw it.

Congratulations you have finished your first 90 days of school!

Certificate

This certificate certifies that _____

(name)

Has completed Book 1 of A Christian Delight Directed Curriculum completing 90 days of _____

(Grade)

Parents Signature_____

Date_____

Copy Right

This curriculum is for your family only please
do not
copy or sell any parts of this book.
Thank You